ALTERNATOR BOOKS™

UNEXPLAINED

GHOULISH GHOSTS

Craig Boutland

Lerner Publications ◆ Minneapolis

Lerner Publications Company
A division of Lerner Publishing Group, Inc.
241 First Avenue North
Minneapolis, MN 55401 USA

For reading levels and more information, look up this title at www.lernerbooks.com.

Main body text set in Minion Pro.
Font provided by Adobe Systems.

Library of Congress Cataloging-in-Publication Data

Names: Boutland, Craig, author.
Title: Ghoulish ghosts / Craig Boutland.
Description: Minneapolis : Lerner Publications, 2019. | Series: Unexplained (Alternator Books) | Includes bibliographical references and index.
Identifiers: LCCN 2018050614 (print) | LCCN 2019006467 (ebook) | ISBN 9781541562882 (eb pdf) | ISBN 9781541562813 (lb : alk. paper) | ISBN 9781541573789 (pb : alk. paper)
Subjects: LCSH: Ghosts—Juvenile literature.
Classification: LCC BF1461 (ebook) | LCC BF1461 .B68 2019 (print) | DDC 133.1—dc23

LC record available at https://lccn.loc.gov/2018050614

Manufactured in the United States of America
1-46407-47497-3/20/2019

Contents

Introduction

Many countries have stories about people who died violently and haunt the living. In Ireland there are stories about banshees, which are spirits of women who have died young. The wailing of the banshee is thought to be a warning that someone is about to die.

Other Worlds?

Almost one-third of Americans believe in ghosts. Why are ghosts and ghost stories so common and so popular? No one really knows. It's impossible to prove that ghosts exist, but some people feel that there are ghosts around them. One wise man in the 1800s explained that death doesn't exist. A person only changes worlds. But can these other worlds really exist?

Ghostly Places

People often claim to have seen ghosts in historic places. There seems to be a link between old buildings and ghosts. This is particularly the case when something bad has happened in a building. Usually, it is because people have died inside.

Haunted buildings can attract many visitors. The Tower of London is an old castle in England. It is said to be haunted by the ghosts of people who were **executed** there. One of the most famous ghosts is that of Anne Boleyn, one of the wives of King Henry VIII. Anne died there in the 1500s. Her ghost has been seen walking toward where she was executed.

Shadowy Figures

Ghosts often take the form of "white ladies" or "gray ladies," like Anne Boleyn in the Tower of London. They are dressed in clothes from the past and walk toward something, ignoring anyone who is watching them. These ghosts do not have a solid physical form. A white lady is almost a person, but not quite.

The Tower of London in England, where Anne Boleyn was beheaded on May 19, 1536.

Ghosts are often seen in graveyards. The most haunted cemetery in the United States is Union Cemetery in Connecticut, which was built in the 1700s. A white lady has been seen among the graves. Who is she? Some people think she is searching for her dead child. Other people say that she was murdered and has returned to haunt the graveyard.

Mystery Lights

Dudleytown, also in Connecticut, was built in the 1740s. The town was abandoned in the 1800s. No one has lived there since. Visitors to the town claimed to have videos showing ghostly glowing circles of light. Rumors spread that the town was haunted. Because of the number of people who came to see Dudleytown's mysterious lights, it has been closed to visitors.

People often claim to see spooky, unexplainable things in old buildings and other **abandoned** places. What is it about these places that attract ghosts or make them appear? Some people think these ghosts have become part of the place and can never leave. They are trapped by the memory of the bad things that happened to them there.

Ghostly History

Some people say they have seen ghosts from historic events. There have been ghost sightings at battlefields. Is this because the ghosts of people who died haunt them? It could be that people visiting the battlefields are thinking about the history around them and imagine they have seen something.

Gettysburg, Pennsylvania is one of the most famous battlefields of the Civil War (1861–1865). Ghost hunters say Gettysburg has powerful connections to the spirit world. People who live there have seen strange orbs of light and white ladies that may have been nurses for wounded soldiers. There are ghost tours of the battlefield where visitors can try to see the ghost of a fallen soldier. Ghosts have also been seen at other Civil War battlefields in Antietam, Maryland, and Chickamunga, Georgia.

The Battle of Antietam took place on September 22, 1862. General Robert E. Lee's Confederate soldiers fought General George McClellan's Union soldiers in a bloody conflict. In just twelve hours, there were some 23,000 casualties, including 3,650 dead.

Millions of soldiers died in World War I (1914–1918). Many of the soldiers' family members reported ghost sightings. Many of the stories were the same. A loved one would suddenly appear at the front door. He would come in and sit down. When the sister, wife, or mother left the room, the soldier disappeared.

A day or so later the family would receive news that their loved one had been killed on the battlefield. Often, he died at exactly the same time as he had appeared at home.

Powerful Energy

Ghost researchers in Britain discovered many similar stories about soldiers returning from the dead. They believed that the emotional pain of millions of men and their families had somehow created a **field** of energy. This energy made the ghosts appear.

Layers of History

Some ghosts are from ancient history. The English city of York was founded by the Romans in about 71 CE. The ghosts of Roman soldiers have been seen marching through the basement of a house that was built in the 1800s. In one detailed **account**, a witness said the ghosts could only be seen from the knees up. They were walking along an old road that in Roman times would have been just over one foot (35 cm) below the basement floor.

In 1881, gravestones were placed on Culloden Moor to mark the graves of the clans.

Ghostly Ground

On April 16, 1746, the last battle fought in Britain took place at Culloden Moor. This place in northern Scotland has many graves of Highland soldiers, or **clansmen**. Most of them were killed by members of enemy clans. They were buried in groups. On April 16 each year, local people report hearing the clash of swords, war cries, and screams of pain. Could these be the ghosts of the clansmen?

Ghosts From Around the World

Ghosts have been seen all over the world. Most sightings are of people who died a painful death or were not properly buried. In Britain, people who killed themselves could not be buried in a cemetery. Because they were not buried in holy ground, people believed their souls would wander the earth forever. Instead, their bodies were buried at crossroads. The sign of the cross was supposed to stop them from coming back as ghosts.

The ancient Romans also believed that people might come back as ghosts if they had not been given a proper burial. They believed the dead became evil spirits called lemures. On May 9, 11, and 13, the Romans performed a ceremony. The oldest man in the house rose from his bed at midnight. He walked through the house, scattering black beans behind him. The ancient Romans thought the lemures would then return to the spirit world.

In Ireland, legend says a headless horseman gallops along country roads at night. Riding a black **stallion**, he carries his own head in his hands. He sometimes holds his head above his body so that he can see for miles. Ghost hunters believe that this headless horseman comes from early Irish history. Up until 600 CE, human victims were **sacrificed** to the god of the harvest. They were often beheaded. Perhaps one of these ghosts has returned.

It is said that if the headless horseman calls a person's name, that person will die.

Part of a woodblock print by Japanese artist Utagawa Kuniyoshi shows a giant skeleton attacking warring noblemen.

Japanese Legend

The Japanese have a legend that says huge ghostly beings made from skeletons walk country roads after dark. These are the skeletons of people who died in ancient battles and were not buried. They come back as angry ghosts because they did not have proper burials. They are looking for their old lives.

Ghosts in Southeast Asia

Bhoots are ghosts that people have seen in India. They are the spirits of people who cannot be reborn into a new life or who have not gone to an afterlife. Instead, they are trapped on earth. Like European or North American ghosts, they often wear white and float above the ground. Some hang in trees. Bhoots sometimes appear as animals. One thing that always gives bhoots away is that their feet point backward.

In Malaysia, some people believe that the human soul is a small being about the size of a thumb. The soul can move and sometimes leave a person's body. When a person dies, the soul leaves the body forever. For seven days it haunts the grave where the person is buried. Then it tries to find another home.

However, some souls never find another home. If a mother dies while giving birth, her soul becomes an evil ghost. The ghost dresses in green and has long hair and fingernails. These ghosts sometimes attack other women.

Contacting Ghosts

For people who believe in ghosts, it can be important to be able to talk to the spirits. The goal is to find out what they want. Helping ghosts get what they want may stop them from frightening or attacking other people. In the Middle Ages, many people believed witches could talk to ghosts. These witches might make ghosts appear using magic.

In the late 1800s, people in Europe began to try to contact ghosts through people called mediums. Mediums claim to be able to communicate with dead people. They ask dead people questions. There are people today who say they have a special understanding of the spirit world. They offer to put people in touch with their dead loved ones. However, many mediums have been proven to be **frauds.** They see a chance to make money from people who are upset.

Hungry Ghost Festival

In China, people believe ghosts can be powerful. It is important to show them respect. Then the ghosts might help their living relatives. The Hungry Ghost Festival takes place throughout the Chinese-speaking world on the fourteenth or fifteenth day of the seventh month. Front rows in theaters are left empty for ghostly visitors, and offerings to ghostly spirits are left on the streets.

Many people do not believe in ghosts. They think it is silly to believe in them. Other people say ghosts must exist because there are so many ghost stories from all around the world. Researchers try to find out how ghosts are created and what they are made of. They read about ghostly sightings and try to make sense of them. They also talk to people who say they have seen ghosts.

Lanterns float down rivers during the Hungry Ghost Festival. They are meant to help the souls of the dead return to the spirit world.

Sometimes ghosts are jokey and not very scary. For example, millions of ghost masks are sold every year for **Halloween**. There have been funny TV shows with stories about ghosts, such as *Scooby-Doo*. Other TV series or films about ghosts can be very frightening. Even though we know they are films, they make us scared.

Do You Believe in Ghosts?

People try to protect themselves from ghosts in many ways. In India, people sprinkle earth on themselves. In Ireland, the headless horseman can be stopped with a gold coin. In Europe and North America, people may try to find out why a ghost is angry and help it to find peace.

We do not know if ghosts exist. But we do know that many people believe in them.

Glossary

abandoned: left alone without people

account: the story a person tells about something that has happened

clansmen: people belonging to a particular tribe or group of people

executed: put to death

field: a space where a certain effect exists

frauds: people who trick other people into believing something, often for money

Halloween: the night of October 31, the eve of All Saints' Day, when ghosts and spirits are believed to appear

rumors: stories that people tell each other, which may or may not be true

sacrificed: killed as a gift to a god or gods

souls: the spiritual parts of human beings or animals, thought to be immortal

stallion: an adult, male horse

Further Information

Big Think: The Science of Ghosts. https://bigthink.com/philip-perry/theres-no-such-thing-as-ghosts-instead-one-of-these-phenomena-is-at-play

How Stuff Works: Ghost Stories. https://people.howstuffworks.com/culture-traditions/holidays-halloween/ghost-stories.htm

Kovacs, Vic. *Haunted Towns and Villages*. New York: Crabtree Publishing Company, 2018.

Pearson, Maggie. *Ghosts and Goblins: Scary Stories from Around the World.* Minneapolis: Darby Creek, 2016.

Seeley, M H. *Freaky Stories About the Paranormal*. New York: Gareth Stevens Publishing, 2016.

Vox: Why People Think They See Ghosts. https://www.vox.com/videos/2017/7/11/15948234/do-ghosts-exist

Wood, Alix. *Haunted Houses*. New York: Gareth Stevens Publishing, 2017.

Index

Photo Acknowledgments

The images inside this book are used with permission of: ©Shutterstock/donates, p. 1; ©iStockphoto.com/Nicolas McComber, p. 4-5; ©Shutterstock/Carlos Caetano, p. 6-7; ©iStockphoto.com/Lawrence Sawyer, p. 8; ©iStockphoto.com/D Keine, p. 9; ©iStockphoto.com/Leo Patrizi, p. 10; ©Shutterstock/Chamille White, p. 11; ©iStockphoto.com/KeeTron, p. 12-13; ©iStockphoto.com/cjp, p. 14; ©Shutterstock/WhiteMocca, p. 15; ©Shutterstock/Serhii Bobyk, p. 16; ©iStockphoto.com/R Peters, p. 17; ©Shutterstock/Olga Kolbakova, p. 18-19; ©Public Domain, p. 20; ©Public Domain/Petrusbarbygere, p. 21; ©iStockphoto.com/Akshrum Singh, p. 22; ©iStockphoto.com/Baona, p. 23; ©iStockphoto.com/S Dominick, p. 24-25; ©Getty Images/VCG, p. 27; ©iStockphoto.com/Mordolff, p. 28; ©Shutterstock/LarioTus, p. 29.

Front Cover: ©Shutterstock/Tom Tom.

Brown Bear Books has made every attempt to contact the copyright holder. If anyone has any information please contact licensing@brownbear.co.uk